NATIONAL FOOTBALL LEAGUE
SUPER BOWL STORIES

★ ★ ★ ★ ★ ★ ★ ★ ★ ★ ★ ★ ★ ★

by Tim Polzer

SCHOLASTIC INC.

New York   Toronto   London   Auckland   Sydney
Mexico City   New Delhi   Hong Kong   Buenos Aires

All photos © Getty Images.
Front Cover: Andy Lyons • Interior: (3) Frank Micelotta; (4) Rick Stewart, George Rose; (5) Jonathan Daniel;
(6) Archie Carpenter, Harry How; (7) Jonathon Daniel, Harry How; (8) Getty Images, Scott Cunningham;
(9) Scott Cunningham, Frank Micelotta; (10) Jamie Squire, Andy Lyons; (11) Brian Bahr, Rick Stewart;
(12, 13) Mike Powell; (14) Getty Images, David Paul Morris; (15) Doug Benc; (16) Mike Powell, Al Bello;
(17) Doug Pensinger (both); (18) George Rose (both); (19) George Rose; (20) Getty Images, Scott Cunningham;
(21) Getty Images, Jonathan Daniel; (22) Rick Stewart, Mike Powell; (23) Simon Bruty, Jonathan Daniel;
(25) Doug Pensinger, Jonathan Daniel; (26) Eliot J. Schechter; (27) Doug Pensinger, Donald Miralle;
(28) Nick Laham, Jed Jacobsohn; (29) Nick Laham, Eliot J. Schechter; (30) Jonathan Daniel, Eliot J. Schechter

INTRODUCTION

When you watch the television broadcasts of National Football League games, have you ever wondered why the networks use so many former players and coaches as analysts? It is because the men who once played and coached the game can share their experiences and the knowledge they collected during their careers on the field.

Who better than quarterbacks like Troy Aikman, Terry Bradshaw, or Steve Young to tell you, the viewer, how well a quarterback is playing and why?

And viewers questioning the play-calling of their favorite team's coach can look to television analysts like Mike Ditka or Jimmy Johnson to explain the choices based on their own experiences.

These former players and coaches are able to evaluate today's players and coaches because their own NFL experiences included both wins and losses. These highs and lows taught them unforgettable lessons and placed them among the league's legends.

This book tells the stories behind some of their biggest games and triumphs.

SUPER BOWL XXVII

TROY AIKMAN
JIMMY JOHNSON
MICHAEL IRVIN

On January 30, 1993, the night before Troy Aikman's first Super Bowl appearance, the fourth-year quarterback knew exactly how the Dallas Cowboys could win their first NFL championship in 15 years. After watching films of the Buffalo Bills in preparation for the game, Troy visited the hotel rooms of each of his offensive linemen to share his discovery. Troy told each of them that if the Cowboys' offensive line could protect him from Buffalo's pass rush, giving him enough time to complete passes to his receivers, Dallas couldn't be beaten.

His prediction was more private than the guarantee his coach, Jimmy Johnson, had made two weeks earlier. Two days before the Cowboys were to host the San Francisco 49ers in the NFC Championship Game, Jimmy called a Dallas-area sports talk radio show and guaranteed that his team would win.

Jimmy was right, and so was Troy. The Cowboys beat the 49ers, earning a spot in the team's first Super Bowl in 15 years. And when the Bills couldn't pressure the Cowboys' quarterback, Troy picked apart the Buffalo defense with pinpoint passes.

Before a crowd of 98,374 at Rose Bowl Stadium in Pasadena, California, Troy threw two touchdown passes to receiver Michael Irvin — just 18 seconds apart — and another to tight end Jay Novacek in the first half. He later clinched a 52–17 victory with a 45-yard touchdown pass to receiver Alvin Harper. In all, Troy completed 22 of 30 pass attempts for 273 yards and no interceptions. The performance earned him the game's Most Valuable Player award. Just four years after the Cowboys drafted Troy with the first pick of the 1989 draft, and after finishing 1–15 in his rookie season, the quarterback from Henryetta, Oklahoma, had led his team to a Super Bowl championship. "It's as great a feeling as I've ever had in my life," Troy said. "I wish every player could experience it."

Super Bowl XXVII MVP honors easily could have gone to Troy's favorite target. Michael Irvin caught 6 passes for 114 yards and 2 touchdowns — the fastest pair of touchdowns by one player in Super Bowl history.

Jimmy Johnson became the first man to play for a national college champion (University of Arkansas in 1964), coach a national college champion (University of Miami, 1987), and coach a Super Bowl champion.

"We said all year that the best game we were going to play was the last game," Jimmy said, "and we saved the best for last."

One year later, Jimmy would lead the Cowboys to a second straight championship with another win over the Buffalo Bills in Super Bowl XXVIII. Troy and Michael would go on to lead the Cowboys to a victory in Super Bowl XXX — for an NFL-record three championships in four seasons.

Troy's 90 victories with the Cowboys in the 1990s made him the winningest starting quarterback of any decade in NFL history. His career statistics include 32,942 passing yards and a passer rating of 81.6. He still holds a Super Bowl record with a 70-percent completion ratio.

Troy was inducted into the Pro Football Hall of Fame in 2006.

SUPER BOWL XL

JEROME BETTIS

Entering the 2005–6 NFL season, Jerome Bettis, whose nickname is "The Bus," knew that he was probably facing the end of the road. The big-bodied running back, who got his nickname because he looked like a school bus when he wore the black-and-gold Pittsburgh Steelers uniform, knew that he had only one more chance to earn an elusive prize — a Super Bowl ring.

Jerome joined the Steelers just a few months after they lost to the Dallas Cowboys in Super Bowl XXX. During the next 10 years, he rushed for 10,571 yards, becoming the NFL's fifth all-time leading rusher with 13,662 yards. But in all that time, neither the Bus nor the Steelers managed to make it to the Super Bowl.

That unfortunate streak showed no signs of ending. In 2005–6 the Steelers failed to defend their AFC North division championship. But Pittsburgh did advance to the AFC playoffs as a wild-card team. The Steelers weren't out of the hunt for a Super Bowl berth, but the odds were against their defeating heavily favored teams like the Indianapolis Colts and the Denver Broncos.

Perhaps because it was Jerome's last chance to go to the Super Bowl or because the championship game was being held in his hometown, Detroit, but the player known as the heart and soul of the Steelers was determined to help his team beat the odds. And he did.

The last time Jerome and the Steelers had played in Detroit, it had been a Thanksgiving Day game. Afterward, Jerome had invited the entire Pittsburgh team to his mother's house for dinner. On this trip to Detroit, however, Jerome's mother didn't have to cook. Instead, she watched her son play in his first Super Bowl.

In Super Bowl XL, Jerome contributed 43 yards on 14 carries, but it was his emotional presence that helped lift the Steelers' confidence against the Seattle Seahawks. The Steelers, who entered the game having won four Super Bowls (IX, X, XIII, XIV), finally won their record-tying fifth Super Bowl ring, or as Pittsburgh fans liked to say, "one for the thumb."

In the Steelers' locker room after their 21–10 victory, Jerome let everyone know that he was going to retire on top.

"It's been an incredible ride," Jerome said. "I'm a champion. I think the Bus's last stop is here in Detroit. It's official."

Sucks

SUPER BOWL XIII

TERRY BRADSHAW

Terry Bradshaw of the Pittsburgh Steelers may have started out as a small-town boy from Shreveport, Louisiana, but by the time he took the field for Super Bowl XIII, he was anything but small-time. As Terry finished his eighth NFL season, he already owned two Super Bowl rings and had triggered the Immaculate Reception, one of the league's most famous last-second touchdowns. But surprising as it may seem, Terry still wanted to prove that he was more than just a good quarterback on a very good team.

Terry had spent his entire professional career proving that he was not just a country boy with a funny personality and Southern drawl. He made the big leap from Louisiana Tech to the NFL when the Steelers made him the first player selected in the 1970 draft.

At the time, the Steelers weren't very good, but coach Chuck Noll saw potential in Terry's strong arm and leadership qualities. Even when many Pittsburgh fans thought their new quarterback would turn out to be a bust, Coach Noll stuck with Terry as he adjusted to the professional game.

In the end, Pittsburgh's patience paid off. Terry developed into a winning quarterback, whether handing the ball to running back Franco Harris or throwing passes to receiver Lynn Swann.

He even called his own plays while leading the Steelers to their first Super Bowl victory in 1975 and then repeated that feat in Super Bowl X. His teammates Harris and Swann were named Most Valuable Player in those games, respectively.

In Super Bowl XIII, Terry had one of his finest days ever, throwing a Super Bowl–record 4 touchdowns and recording a personal-best 318 yards on just 17 completions.

"I was surprised at how relaxed I was," Terry said. "I was able to stay relaxed and not worry so much."

Bradshaw's passing proved to be the difference in the Steelers' 35–31 win over the Dallas Cowboys, and he was presented with his first Super Bowl MVP award.

The following year, Terry was named MVP again, this time in the Steelers' 31–19 victory over the Los Angeles Rams in Super Bowl XIV. He was inducted into the Pro Football Hall of Fame in 1989.

SUPER BOWL XXXII

TERRELL DAVIS

The first Super Bowl of Terrell Davis's professional career was unforgettable for many reasons. First, the game was being played in his hometown, San Diego. When the game started, he had to overcome a painful migraine. When it was over, he had been named Most Valuable Player and had helped an NFL legend realize a Super Bowl dream.

In 15 years with the Denver Broncos, John Elway had become known as one of the game's best all-time quarterbacks, passing, scrambling, and leading his team to many come-from-behind wins. But as John's Hall of Fame–caliber career was winding down, he had yet to win a Super Bowl — even after three attempts. But that was before Terrell Davis joined the Broncos.

Terrell was selected with the 196th pick in the 1995 NFL Draft, and the rookie from Georgia made the Broncos' management look like geniuses when he rushed for 1,117 yards. In doing so, Terrell became the lowest-drafted player to rush for 1,000 yards as a rookie, and the first Bronco to surpass 1,000 yards in four seasons.

More importantly, Terrell's 300-plus carries and explosiveness caused defenses to divide their attention between the Broncos' running attack and John Elway's passing game.

Previously, John hadn't had the opportunity to play with such an outstanding running back. Terrell's presence on the field helped John to open up his game and become even more lethal.

Terrell was so excited about playing in his first Super Bowl, that on game day he forgot to take medication for a condition that causes him to suffer painful migraine headaches. He took the medication just before kickoff, but he was worried that it would not take effect until late in the game.

Broncos fans grew concerned when the Green Bay Packers scored early, and found something else to worry about when they lost their star running back. In the second quarter, Terrell was kicked in the head. His vision affected, he was forced to retreat to the locker room and wait for his painful headache to subside. But when the second half began, Terrell was ready for action.

"I was back in business . . . refreshed, and with my vision even better than before, crystal clear," Terrell said. "I had a second chance, and I was going to take complete advantage of it."

With the teams tied 24–24, the Broncos called on Terrell. His third touchdown with less than two minutes remaining proved to be the game-winning score. For his efforts, Terrell was named the MVP of Super Bowl XXXII.

But one Super Bowl ring was not enough for Terrell and John. One year later, in Super Bowl XXXIII, they did it again. Terrell rushed for 102 yards and John was voted MVP in the final game of his career.

SUPER BOWL XX

MIKE DITKA

Mike Ditka was the perfect man to coach the 1985 Chicago Bears. The man known as "Iron Mike" confidently led a cast of bigger-than-life characters through one of the NFL's most dominating regular-season runs and did not ease up in Super Bowl XX.

Mike's team included outspoken quarterback Jim McMahon, who sported a Mohawk and wrote messages on his headbands, and humungous William "The Refrigerator" Perry, a 300-plus–pound defensive tackle who liked to line up at running back near the goal line. Some Bears players even recorded a music video, singing and dancing to "The Super Bowl Shuffle."

Mike's intensity as a coach — he once broke his hand punching a blackboard to stress a point — was well known. It matched his reputation from his playing days, when he rumbled across the field as one of the NFL's toughest tight ends.

Mike was drafted by the Bears in 1961 and made an immediate impact on the position and the offensive philosophy. Professional tight ends were considered blockers until Mike had 56 receptions as a rookie, helping to transform the position into a passing weapon. His personality fit the rough-and-tumble Bears persona created by one of NFL's founders and Chicago owner/coach George "Papa Bear" Halas.

During Mike's fourth season as head coach in Chicago, the Bears' "46 Zone" defense was one of the best in NFL history, and after winning its first 12 games, the team appeared capable of matching the 1972 Miami Dolphins' perfect 17–0 season. The Dolphins upset the Bears 38–24 to end their streak, but it would be the Bears' only loss. They finished 16–1 and were heavily favored to beat the Patriots in Super Bowl XX.

After the Patriots kicked a field goal just 1:19 into the game for the quickest lead in Super Bowl history, the Bears' defense tightened up while their offense exploded for 23 first-half points. The Bears managed to score another 23 points in the second half to put the game away with a then–Super Bowl record 46 points. Afterward, Mike thanked his late Chicago mentor.

"What you do in life by yourself doesn't mean as much as what you accomplish with a group of people," Mike said. "It's because of Mr. Halas that I'm here. I'm just trying to pay some dues."

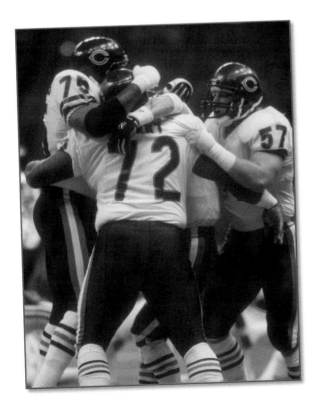

SUPER BOWL XI

JOHN MADDEN

Today John Madden may be best known for his NFL broadcast talents and famous video-game series. But there was a time when he had to prove that he could win big games and coach the Oakland Raiders to a Super Bowl championship.

In 1967, Raiders owner Al Davis hired the 32-year-old as one of the youngest head coaches in pro football history, and John immediately made an impact. In his first year, he led the team to a 12–1–1 record. He would go on to coach the Raiders for 10 seasons while becoming one of the most successful coaches in NFL history. John's .759 regular-season winning percentage still ranks as the highest among coaches with at least 100 career victories, and the Raiders never had a losing record with John as their head coach.

But despite John's regular-season success, the Raiders struggled in the playoffs and found themselves falling short of a championship. After losing the AFC Championship Game five times in seven years, critics said the team could not win the big one.

In 1976, John and the Raiders were determined to prove the skeptics wrong. For the third straight season, the Raiders faced the Pittsburgh Steelers in the AFC Championship Game for the right to play in Super Bowl XI.

This time, John and the Raiders came out on top, defeating the Steelers 24–7, for their twelfth victory in a row.

In Super Bowl XI, the Raiders took to the field in Rose Bowl Stadium to face the Minnesota Vikings before a television audience of 81 million viewers, then the largest audience ever to watch a sporting event.

When the Raiders' offense stalled, then missed a field goal in the first quarter, John shouted at his quarterback, Kenny Stabler. The Raiders coach was concerned that the team might need those points before the game was over. Kenny told his coach not to worry. "There's plenty more points out there for us," Kenny said. He was right. Oakland scored on three consecutive possessions in the second quarter for a 16–0 halftime lead.

John's strategy of calling play-action passes on first down kept the Vikings' highly rated defense off balance, allowing the Raiders to keep scoring. When the game ended, the Raiders had defeated the Vikings 32–14, while producing a record-breaking 429 yards of total offense. And John had proved that he could win a big game.

"They can't say anymore that we don't win the big one. Super Bowl XI is ours, and 10 or 20 years from now Super Bowl XI will still be ours," John said. "I'll never take off the Super Bowl ring. It's something I will always cherish."

SUPER BOWL XXIX

DEION SANDERS

After losing back-to-back NFC Championship Games to the Dallas Cowboys in 1992 and 1993, the San Francisco 49ers needed a bold plan. How could they slow down the Cowboys' explosive offense without trading away valuable players and going over the salary cap?

The 49ers found their answer: Deion Sanders. The Pro Bowl cornerback known by nicknames such as "Prime Time" and "Neon" signed a free-agent contract with the team.

If Deion felt the heavy pressure of beating Dallas and leading the 49ers to the Super Bowl, he did not show it. He played like his usual confident self, and made a bigger impact than even the 49ers could imagine.

Despite missing the first week, Deion had perhaps his best season as a professional football player, grabbing 6 interceptions and returning them for an NFL-best 303 yards and 3 touchdowns. For his performance, he was named the NFL's Defensive Player of the Year.

Deion also solved the 49ers' Cowboy problem, limiting All-Pro receiver Michael Irvin during the teams' regular-season match and in the NFC Championship Game.

In 1995, Deion made more history just by stepping on the field. After playing major league baseball with the New York Yankees, Atlanta Braves, and Cincinnati Reds, Deion became the only athlete to have played in both a Super Bowl and a World Series when he and the 49ers took the field against the San Diego Chargers.

The 49ers quickly jumped out to a lead over the Chargers, and when San Diego responded by pushing deep into San Francisco territory, Deion intercepted a Gale Gilbert pass in the end zone to end the drive with less than 10 minutes remaining in the game.

A few minutes later, the almost 75,000 spectators in Miami's Joe Robbie Stadium were given another treat, when Deion lined up at receiver. Midway through the fourth quarter, Steve Young saw Deion streaking on a deep pattern and threw the football his way, only to have the ball knocked away by Chargers safety Stanley Richards.

Deion may not have caught a pass, but he did the job he was hired to do: help the 49ers get over the hump and win their fifth Super Bowl, 49–26.

The next season, Dallas took a cue from San Francisco and signed Deion. Deion would win back-to-back Super Bowls as a Cowboy.

SUPER BOWL XXI

PHIL SIMMS

On January 25, 1987, a quarterback from little Morehead State University in Kentucky found himself in the spotlight of Super Bowl XXI, about to take the field in front of 101,063 spectators at Rose Bowl Stadium. A lot of players might have been nervous, but Phil Simms did not even blink. After all, if he could play quarterback in New York City, he could play anywhere.

Simms was something of an unknown when the New York Giants selected him in the first round of the 1979 draft. Confused Giants fans reacted to his selection with boos.

Phil quickly turned those boos to cheers when he passed for 1,743 yards and was named to the NFL All-Rookie team. Still some New York fans wondered if his many interceptions would keep the Giants from winning a Super Bowl championship. In his seventh NFL season, Phil had a chance to set the Big Apple — and NFL fans — straight.

Against the Denver Broncos, Phil produced the greatest display of precision passing in Super Bowl history, completing a record 22 of 25 passes.

With the Giants trailing 10–9 at halftime, Phil caught fire, going a perfect 10 of 10 while leading New York to a Super Bowl record 30 second-half points. The Giants' 24 unanswered points put the game out of reach and gave the team its first Super Bowl title.

In leading the Giants to a 39–20 victory, Phil passed for 268 yards and 3 touchdowns, and was voted the game's Most Valuable Player.

After the game, Phil provided another first, becoming the first Super Bowl MVP to say, "I'm going to Disneyland!"

SUPER BOWL XVII

JOE THEISMANN

In 1983, Washington Redskins quarterback Joe Theismann was on the verge of proving people wrong again. Joe, who had gone so far as to leave the country rather than sign with the Miami Dolphins and give up his dream of playing quarterback, was set to take the field against those same Dolphins in Super Bowl XVII.

Joe had taken a long road to get back to the NFL. When the Dolphins drafted the Notre Dame quarterback, and runner-up for college football's Heisman Trophy, in the fourth round of the 1971 NFL Draft, some skeptics thought Joe was too short to see beyond the pocket and would make a better rusher than passer. Joe didn't believe the Dolphins would stick with him at quarterback, so he took his talents to the Toronto Argonauts of the Canadian Football League. The Argonauts would let him play quarterback.

While the NFL watched from afar, the CFL rookie quickly developed his skills, leading the Argonauts to a 10–4 record and finishing atop the CFL's Eastern Conference passing statistics.

In 1974, the Redskins took a chance and obtained Joe's rights, bringing him onto their roster as a backup to quarterbacks Sonny Jurgenson and Billy Kilmer. In fact, Joe got most of his playing time as a punt returner until his fifth season, when he took over as quarterback.

In 1983, a season shortened by a players' strike, Joe led the Redskins to an 8–1 record and one of the most dominating postseason streaks, in which Washington outscored its three NFC playoff opponents 83–31, including a decisive 31–17 victory over the Dallas Cowboys in the NFC Championship Game.

In Super Bowl XVII, the Redskins faced the favored Dolphins, whose "Killer Bees" defense was one of the NFL's best. When Joe threw a 4-yard touchdown pass to Alvin Garret with less than two minutes left in the second quarter, the Redskins figured to enter halftime with a 10–10 tie. But the Dolphins' Fulton Walker returned the ensuing kickoff for a touchdown — the first in Super Bowl history — giving the Dolphins a 17–10 lead at halftime.

Joe and the Redskins knew they had just 30 more minutes to regain the lead if they were going to win the team's first NFL championship since 1942. The Redskins responded, scoring 17 unanswered points in the second half, including a touchdown pass from Joe to Charlie Brown, to pull away from the Dolphins and give Joe his one and only Super Bowl ring.

Afterward, Joe pinched himself to make sure he was not dreaming.

"Winning the Super Bowl was genuinely a dream come true," Joe said.

SUPER BOWL XXIX

STEVE YOUNG

Before Super Bowl XXIX in Miami, Steve Young was asked why he was smiling. "This is fun now," he said. Those who had followed Steve's development leading up to the biggest game of his career knew exactly why Steve was having fun: He was about to step out of the shadow of one of the greatest quarterbacks in NFL history.

Steve was already one of the NFL's most athletic quarterbacks when he was traded to the San Francisco 49ers in 1987. The 49ers signed him to back up the team's most famous Super Bowl hero, Joe Montana.

After playing sparingly during his first four seasons with the 49ers, Steve finally got his chance to shine when injuries sidelined Joe for much of 1991 and 1992. Steve responded by posting a league-high 101.8 passer rating and the first of his four straight NFL passing titles.

When the team decided to install Steve as its permanent starting quarterback, Joe asked for a trade and joined the Kansas City Chiefs. The 49ers now were Steve's team, but the team's fans were used to winning Super Bowls. When the team fell short under Steve, fans jumped to the conclusion that he was at fault, no matter how well he had played. He would not make San Francisco fans forget Joe until he proved that he could win a Super Bowl.

His best season occurred in 1994 when Steve led the 49ers to a 13–3 record and the NFC West title. In the NFC Championship Game, Steve threw 2 touchdowns and rushed for another against the Dallas Cowboys, who had stopped the 49ers short of the Super Bowl the previous two seasons. But not this year. This year the 49ers were going to the Super Bowl in Miami.

"Before, I was pressing so hard, trying to outdistance criticism and skepticism. It just got sickening," Steve said.

Now Steve had to beat the San Diego Chargers to reach his goal of winning the Super Bowl and silencing his critics. With the world watching, Steve quickly staked his claim, throwing a 44-yard touchdown pass to Jerry Rice on the game's third play. The 49ers would never trail.

Steve completed 24 of 36 passes for 325 yards and 6 touchdowns in the 49ers' 49–26 win. He also rushed for 49 yards, becoming the first player to finish the Super Bowl as the game's leading passer and rusher. Steve was voted the game's Most Valuable Player and would later be elected to the Pro Football Hall of Fame — just like his former teammate, Joe Montana.

SUPER BOWL XLI

INDIANAPOLIS COLTS
VS.
CHICAGO BEARS

There were many firsts surrounding Super Bowl XLI, which pitted the Indianapolis Colts against the Chicago Bears at Dolphin Stadium in Miami, Florida. History was made before the teams ever stepped on the field when Indianapolis's Tony Dungy and Chicago's Lovie Smith became the first African-American head coaches to lead their teams into a Super Bowl. But there was more to come as the game got underway.

Chicago's first Super Bowl appearance in 21 years got off to an exciting start when the Bears' Devin Hester returned the opening kickoff 92 yards for a touchdown and an early lead. Hester's touchdown return was the first ever on a Super Bowl's opening kickoff and the quickest score in Super Bowl history.

The Colts, making their first Super Bowl appearance since 1971, were forced to mount an early comeback in challenging weather conditions. As storm clouds hovered over the stadium, Super Bowl XLI became the first Super Bowl played entirely in the rain, but the wet conditions did not slow Indianapolis down.

Trailing 7–0, the Colts looked to their quarterback, Peyton Manning, to bring them back. The nine-year veteran entered his first Super Bowl owning many NFL passing records, but no championship ring. Despite having to throw a wet football through the downpour and high winds, Manning remained calm and on target, completing 25 of 38 passes for 247 yards and a 53-yard touchdown to Reggie Wayne in the first quarter.

Bears quarterback Rex Grossman did not fare as well as Manning. Though he completed 20 of 28 passes, he also threw two interceptions and dropped two snaps, one that resulted in a turnover.

Once the Colts regained the lead in the second quarter they never looked back. The Indianapolis offense relied on running backs Dominic Rhodes and rookie Joseph Addai to control the ball and time of possession. This duo combined for 190 yards rushing against the top-rated Bears defense, and took some of the pressure off of Manning in the pass pocket.

Not to be outdone, the Colts' defense limited the Bears to just one offensive touchdown and caused four turnovers including a 56-yard interception that was returned by Kelvin Hayden for a game-clinching touchdown.

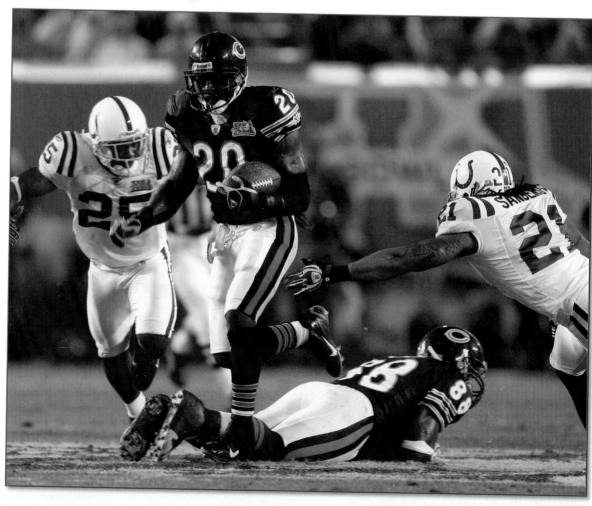

The Colts even made special teams history of their own when kicker Adam Vinatieri converted three field goals to set a new Super Bowl record for career field goals.

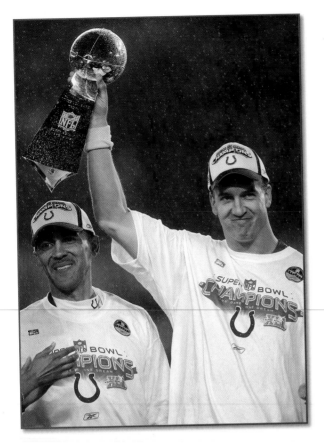

With a 29–17 victory, the Indianapolis Colts earned their own place in Super Bowl history. For his efforts, quarterback Peyton Manning was voted the Most Valuable Player of Super Bowl XLI, but he was quick to acknowledge that the award could have gone to one of several other teammates. "That's been our theme all year, we have won as a team," he said.

SUPER BOWL STATS

Super Bowl	Date	Teams	Most Valuable Player
XLI	Feb. 4, 2007	Indianapolis 29, Chicago 17	Peyton Manning
XL	Feb. 5, 2006	Pittsburgh 21, Seattle 10	Hines Ward
XXXIX	Feb. 6, 2005	New England 24, Philadelphia 21	Deion Branch
XXXVIII	Feb. 1, 2004	New England 32, Carolina 29	Tom Brady
XXXVII	Jan. 26, 2003	Tampa Bay 48, Oakland 21	Dexter Jackson
XXXVI	Feb. 3, 2002	New England 20, St. Louis 17	Tom Brady
XXXV	Jan. 28, 2001	Baltimore 34, N.Y. Giants 7	Ray Lewis
XXXIV	Jan. 30, 2000	St. Louis 23, Tennessee 16	Kurt Warner
XXXIII	Jan. 31, 1999	Denver 34, Atlanta 19	John Elway
XXXII	Jan. 25, 1998	Denver 31, Green Bay 24	Terrell Davis
XXXI	Jan. 26, 1997	Green Bay 35, New England 21	Desmond Howard
XXX	Jan. 28, 1996	Dallas 27, Pittsburgh 17	Larry Brown
XXIX	Jan. 29, 1995	San Francisco 49, San Diego 26	Steve Young
XXVIII	Jan. 30, 1994	Dallas 30, Buffalo 13	Emmitt Smith
XXVII	Jan. 31, 1993	Dallas 52, Buffalo 17	Troy Aikman
XXVI	Jan. 26, 1992	Washington 37, Buffalo 24	Mark Rypien
XXV	Jan. 27, 1991	N.Y. Giants 20, Buffalo 19	Ottis Anderson
XXIV	Jan. 28, 1990	San Francisco 55, Denver 10	Joe Montana
XXIII	Jan. 22, 1989	San Francisco 20, Cincinnati 16	Jerry Rice
XXII	Jan. 31, 1988	Washington 42, Denver 10	Doug Williams
XXI	Jan. 25, 1987	N.Y. Giants 39, Denver 20	Phil Simms

SUPER BOWL STATS

Super Bowl	Date	Teams	Most Valuable Player
XX	Jan. 26, 1986	Chicago 46, New England 10	Richard Dent
XIX	Jan. 20, 1985	San Francisco 38, Miami 16	Joe Montana
XVIII	Jan. 22, 1984	L.A. Raiders 38, Washington 9	Marcus Allen
XVII	Jan. 30, 1983	Washington 27, Miami 17	John Riggins
XVI	Jan. 24, 1982	San Francisco 26, Cincinnati 21	Joe Montana
XV	Jan. 25, 1981	Oakland 27, Philadelphia 10	Jim Plunkett
XIV	Jan. 20, 1980	Pittsburgh 31, L.A. Rams 19	Terry Bradshaw
XIII	Jan. 21, 1979	Pittsburgh 35, Dallas 31	Terry Bradshaw
XII	Jan. 15, 1978	Dallas 27, Denver 10	Randy White, Harvey Martin
XI	Jan. 9, 1977	Oakland 32, Minnesota 14	Fred Biletnikoff
X	Jan. 18, 1976	Pittsburgh 21, Dallas 17	Lynn Swann
IX	Jan. 12, 1975	Pittsburgh 16, Minnesota 14	Franco Harris
VIII	Jan. 13, 1974	Miami 24, Minnesota 7	Larry Csonka
VII	Jan. 14, 1973	Miami 14, Washington 7	Jake Scott
VI	Jan. 16, 1972	Dallas 24, Miami 3	Roger Staubach
V	Jan. 17, 1971	Baltimore 16, Dallas 13	Chuck Howley
IV	Jan. 11, 1970	Kansas City 23, Minnesota 7	Len Dawson
III	Jan. 12, 1969	N.Y. Jets 16, Baltimore 7	Joe Namath
II	Jan. 14, 1968	Green Bay 33, Oakland 14	Bart Starr
I	Jan. 15, 1967	Green Bay 35, Kansas City 10	Bart Starr